National Parks
Mount Rainier

JOANNE MATTERN

Children's Press®
An Imprint of Scholastic Inc.

Content Consultant
James Gramann, PhD
Professor Emeritus, Department of Recreation, Park and Tourism Sciences
Texas A&M University, College Station, Texas

Library of Congress Cataloging-in-Publication Data
A CIP catalog record for this book is available from the Library of Congress
ISBN 9780531175941 (library binding) ISBN 9780531189993 (pbk.)

All rights reserved. Published in 2019 by Children's Press, an imprint of Scholastic Inc.
Printed in Heshan, China 62

SCHOLASTIC, CHILDREN'S PRESS, A TRUE BOOK™, and associated logos are trademarks and/or
registered trademarks of Scholastic Inc.

Scholastic Inc., 557 Broadway, New York, NY 10012

1 2 3 4 5 6 7 8 9 10 R 28 27 26 25 24 23 22 21 20 19

Front cover (main): Mount Rainier
Front cover (inset): Skier
Back cover: Mountain goat

Find the Truth!

Everything you are about to read is true *except* for one of the sentences on this page.

Which one is **TRUE**?

T or F   Peter Rainier named the park after himself.

T or F   Some trees in the park are almost 1,000 years old.

Find the answers in this book.

Contents

THE BIG TRUTH!

National Parks Field Guide: Mount Rainier

Mountain goat

Mount Rainier

Rock climber

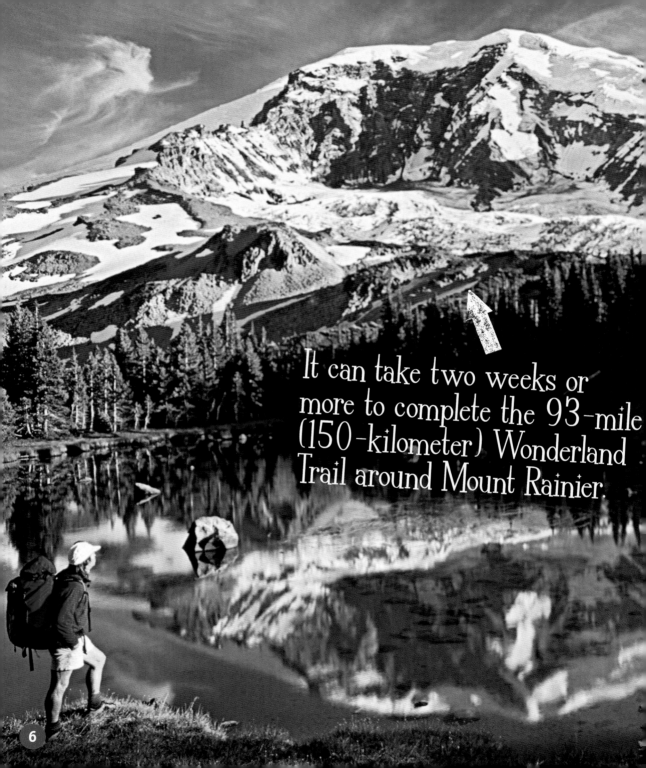

It can take two weeks or more to complete the 93-mile (150-kilometer) Wonderland Trail around Mount Rainier.

CHAPTER 1

A Majestic Mountain

You can see Mount Rainier towering over western Washington State from miles away. The snowcapped mountain is a breathtaking sight. As you gaze on the mountain, you are also looking at one of the United States' most beautiful national parks.

Mount Rainier National Park is a special place. The mountain at its heart is in fact a **dormant** volcano. And yet it is also home to frozen **glaciers**. It has rivers, lakes, and even hot springs!

Mount Rainier
National Park

First Settlers

Fifteen thousand years ago, thick ice and snow covered all of Mount Rainier year-round. Early human settlers lived in the area's plains and valleys. Researchers have found **artifacts** these people left behind, including stone scrapers and arrowheads.

About 9,000 years ago, much of the ice and snow had melted. Native American groups began moving onto the slopes. They called the peak Takhoma. Groups hunted animals and gathered berries and other foods in the region.

Ancestors of the Yakama were one of several Native American groups to live in what is now Washington. Many Yakama still live there today.

Captain George Vancouver mapped much of North America's Pacific coastline.

New Explorers

The first European to see Mount Rainier was Captain George Vancouver of the British Royal Navy. In 1792, Vancouver was sailing along the Pacific coast, making maps. He named the mountain after his friend, Rear Admiral Peter Rainier. The name remains, though Rainier never saw the mountain.

As word of the mountain spread, more explorers came to see it. Many tried to reach the summit. The first recorded success among these newcomers was in 1870.

Making a Park

In 1883, a white settler named James Longmire built a hotel and spa at a mineral spring on the mountain. It attracted visitors who came to bathe in the spring.

Tourism grew. By 1893, many groups were working to protect the land. In 1899, Mount Rainier became the country's fifth national park.

A Timeline of Mount Rainier National Park

About 13,000 BCE
The first humans arrive in the area around Mount Rainier.

About 7000 BCE
Groups including ancestors of the Nisqually, Puyallup, and Yakama move to the area.

1792 CE
Captain George Vancouver is the first European to see the mountain.

Growing Pains

The park quickly became crowded. In 1906, nearly 2,000 people visited the park. That figure shot up to nearly 35,000 in 1915. Park workers struggled to keep up. They built new roads and places to stay.

Mount Rainier was the first national park to allow cars. Afterward, traffic to the park increased even more. Many park rangers spent much of their time directing traffic.

1870

P. B. Van Trump and General Hazard Stevens complete the first recorded successful climb of Mount Rainier.

1899

Mount Rainier becomes the fifth national park in the United States.

1907

Mount Rainier becomes the first national park officially open to cars.

2017

More than 1.4 million people visit the park.

Building a Better Park

The park underwent many improvements during the first half of the 20th century. Workers built more roads and trails, improved campgrounds, and added parking lots. They also installed a golf course. Rangers began leading programs to teach visitors about the area. In later decades, some human-made attractions were closed because they threatened the habitat or suffered poor business. But these changes have not hurt the park's popularity. Each year, more than a million people visit to hike, to camp, and even to climb the mighty peak.

Climbers stop for a photo on Mount Rainier in about 1920.

National Park Fact File

A national park is land that is protected by the federal government. It is a place of importance to the United States because of its beauty, history, or value to scientists. The U.S. Congress creates a national park by passing a law. Here are some key facts about Mount Rainier National Park.

Mount Rainier National Park	
Location	Washington
Year established	1899
Size	369 square miles (956 sq km)
Average number of visitors each year	About 1.2 million
Famous features	Mount Rainier, lava flows, glaciers, ancient forests, ice caves
Highest elevation	The summit of Mount Rainier, at 14,410 feet (4,392 meters)
Largest glacier	Emmons Glacier, at 4.3 square miles (11 sq km)
Oldest rocks	Nearly 40 million years old

There are ice caves beneath the surface of Mount Rainier's crater. They are carved by steam coming from inside the crater.

14

CHAPTER **2**

Fire and Ice

Mount Rainier is more than just a beautiful mountain. It is also a volcano. Although it has not erupted in more than a century, lava, dust, and other **debris** from past eruptions have left their marks. Ice has also helped carve the scenery. Ancient glaciers once covered much of the mountain and surrounding plains and valleys, and many glaciers still remain. As the volcano's fire and the glaciers' ice interacted, they shaped the land into something unique.

A Sleeping Volcano

Mount Rainier is a **composite volcano**. Millions of years of eruptions deposited layers of rock from hardened lava on the mountain's sides. Those layers give the mountain its shape.

The most recent reports of eruptions were in 1895. People said they saw smoke and steam coming from the mountain. Today, Mount Rainier is dormant. There is, however, still activity beneath the surface and scientists expect it to erupt again. They monitor this activity so they can warn of any future eruption.

A researcher adjusts the antenna at a monitoring station that tracks what is happening beneath the surface of Mount Rainier.

Climbing the Mountain

Thousands of adventurers try to reach Mount Rainier's peak every year. The climb is difficult, and fewer than half of all climbers who attempt it succeed. Reaching the summit is thrilling but also dangerous. Climbers face challenges such as thin air, unpredictable weather, icy trails, and possible avalanches. The mountain is also very steep, rising more than 9,000 feet (2,743 m) in only 8 miles (13 km). In 2014, six climbers lost their lives when they fell. In 1981, 11 climbers died in an avalanche.

Volcanic Landscape

Glaciers can stop flowing lava and other volcanic debris in their tracks. In places where this happened during past eruptions, the lava cooled quickly. As it did, it cracked into six-sided shapes called columns.

Hot rock and gases can also melt snow around the volcano, which then flows like an avalanche down the mountain. This is called a **lahar**. A lahar can travel more than 50 miles (80 km) an hour, taking rocks, trees, and mud with it. Past lahars have left this debris piled up along streams and in valleys.

Lava columns may look human-made, but they are entirely natural!

Stone walls were built around this natural spring in Mount Rainier National Park.

Mineral springs form when water from rain and melting snow flows into the ground through cracks in the mountain. Underground, the high temperatures inside the volcano heat the water. The water absorbs minerals from the rocks and mixes with carbon dioxide. Eventually, it bubbles up out of the ground. In the past, visitors sometimes drank the water, believing it was good for their health.

A camper on Curtis Ridge looks out over the bluish Carbon Glacier.

Land of Glaciers

Twenty-five major glaciers remain at Mount Rainier, plus many smaller patches of ice and snow. At 4.3 square miles (11 sq km), Emmons Glacier is the largest U.S. glacier outside of Alaska. Emmons extends down into the White River Valley, which is covered with rocks and debris from the glacier's movement.

The Carbon Glacier has the highest volume of ice of any glacier in the park. This means it contains more ice than other glaciers, even if the ice isn't spread across as large an area of land.

A Glacier Shrinks

One hundred years ago, the Paradise-Stevens Glacier was a big attraction. It was easy to reach and was full of ice caves to explore. But warming temperatures have melted the glacier over the years. By the 1970s, it was less than half the size it had been in 1896, and it has continued to shrink. The rapid melting left behind an area strewn with large rocks and debris. Today, visitors have a rare opportunity to view these rock features, which would otherwise be beneath a glacier.

Large boulders can sometimes be found in areas with glaciers. This one is near Nisqually Glacier.

CHAPTER 3

Wildlife on the Mountain

Mount Rainier National Park has several different **ecosystems,** each of which supports a range of animals. Mammals large and small roam through the park, as birds soar overhead. Visitors might spot a snake slithering silently through the grass or hear the rare yelp of a salamander. Insects buzz through the brush, as fish glide through the water and amphibians nestle nearby.

 Never approach a baby bobcat. Even if it is alone, its mother is probably nearby.

Mammals of All Sizes

Black bears are among the park's largest animals, weighing up to 500 pounds (227 kilograms). As **omnivores**, they eat almost anything. Visitors should never leave food out where bears might follow the smell and come after it.

Smaller mammals include beavers, jumping mice, and seven bat species. Weasel-like fishers were once common. They were trapped for their fur and nearly disappeared in the mid-1900s. But scientists are introducing more fishers into the area, and their numbers are growing.

Black bears are common throughout the park. You might spot them on trails and around camping grounds.

Though spotted owls are nocturnal, you can sometimes see them swooping through the air when it's still light out.

Birds All Around

About 187 species of birds live in the park. Large **predators** include ospreys, eagles, and hawks. These hunters live in trees and swoop down to snatch fish and small animals. Waterbirds such as ducks, gulls, and herons live in lakes and rivers. Other birds stay mainly on the ground. Pheasants, quail, and grouse are among these. Mount Rainier is also home to pigeons, doves, and many different songbirds.

(Left) A northwestern garter snake basks in the sun high in the park. (Above) Pacific giant salamanders are only found in the northwestern United States.

Amphibians and Reptiles

The Pacific giant salamander is one of the park's most unusual residents. One of the estimated 14 amphibians in the park, it measures up to 12 inches (30.5 centimeters) long. It is big enough to eat smaller salamanders, snakes, and even mice. The Pacific giant salamander is also the only salamander that makes sounds. Visitors who listen carefully might hear it yelp! Reptiles in the park include the rubber boa, northern alligator lizard, and several types of garter snakes.

Fish and Insects

In the past, park rangers stocked the streams and lakes with fish. However, that practice stopped about 45 years ago. Today, Mount Rainier's aquatic, or water, habitats are left in their natural state. Salmon and trout thrive in many of Mount Rainier's rivers and streams.

The park's wildflowers attract bumblebees, butterflies, and beetles. Dragonflies flit over the water. Carpenter ants live in dead trees. Everywhere you look, you will find signs of animal life.

Chinook salmon are often found in local bodies of water.

National Parks Field Guide: Mount Rainier

Here are a few of the hundreds of fascinating animals you may see in the park.

Bobcat

Scientific name: *Lynx rufus*

Habitat: Throughout the park's forests

Diet: Woodchucks, rabbits, birds, reptiles

Fact: This nocturnal cat is named for its short, or bobbed, tail.

Cascade red fox

Scientific name: *Vulpes vulpes cascadensis*

Habitat: Higher elevations on the mountain

Diet: Mice, birds, rabbits

Fact: The Cascade red fox only lives high up in the Cascade Mountains.

Mountain goat

Scientific name: *Oreamnos americanus*

Habitat: Mountains and steep rock slopes

Diet: Grasses, mosses, twigs, leaves

Fact: A mountain goat's long white hair keeps it warm and provides camouflage from predators in winter.

Elk

Scientific name: *Cervus canadensis*

Habitat: Lower elevations in fall and winter, higher elevations in spring and summer

Diet: Grasses, leaves, bark

Fact: A male elk's antlers can reach more than 4 feet (1.2 m) in length.

Spotted owl

Scientific name: *Strix occidentalis*

Habitat: Old growth forests

Diet: Rats, mice, birds, insects

Fact: The spotted owl is one of the largest owls in North America.

Common garter snake

Scientific name: *Thamnophis sirtalis*

Habitat: Wet meadows and near water

Diet: Insects, earthworms, frog eggs, tadpoles, mice

Fact: Garter snakes give birth to live young, and a single litter can include as many as 80 babies.

An Abundance of Plants

A variety of ecosystems stretch across Mount Rainier National Park, from valley to summit. Trees, shrubs, flowers, and other plants change depending on elevation, or height above sea level. A hike through the park can include everything from pine forests to grassy meadows. Throughout, visitors can keep an eye out for the more than 1,000 different species of plants.

Forests cover about 58 percent of Mount Rainier National Park.

Down Low and Up High

Almost all the trees in the park are **conifers**. Mount Rainier's lower levels are covered with Douglas fir trees, pines, and cedars.

As visitors travel up the mountain, the forests change. Some trees, such as the mountain hemlock, are more common at higher elevations. Meadows are also found here. During the spring and summer, these meadows fill with color. Wildflowers such as Cascade asters, avalanche lilies, pasqueflowers, and scarlet paintbrushes have a short growing season because of the cold climate. In the highest **alpine** areas, hardy sedges and heather grow in the harsh ecosystem.

Alpine

Clumps of sedges and flowering heather grow in areas that aren't permanently covered in snow and ice.

Dwarf lupine

White mountain heather

Subalpine

Conifers mix with open meadows full of berries and flowering plants.

Mountain hemlock

Huckleberry

Forest

Denser forests cover the lower half of the park, with a variety of firs, pines, spruces, and other trees.

Western red cedar

Pacific silver fir

A relatively easy hike loops through the Grove of the Patriarchs.

One of the most amazing places in the park is the Grove of the Patriarchs, located off Stevens Canyon. Visitors can hike through stands of trees that are almost 1,000 years old. The park's largest trees are found here. There's a cedar that is more than 25 feet (7.6 m) around and a Douglas fir that is more than 35 feet (10.6 m) around. Humans feel tiny in this ancient forest!

Tough Tasks

To keep the ecosystem healthy, rangers and volunteers sometimes remove or introduce plants. This can be tougher than it sounds. **Invasive** plants cause problems for native species and must be destroyed. Workers may spend long days trekking through the wild to track down these invaders. Sometimes, they even rappel down steep slopes to reach the plants they're after.

Areas of the park sometimes suffer serious damage from fire, humans, or other causes. To help these areas recover, workers plant young, native plants, often in hard-to-reach locations. Rangers use helicopters to transport heavy loads of plants safely to their new homes.

Water flows down a cliff created by a glacier at Nisqually Glacier.

CHAPTER 5

Danger in the Park

Mount Rainier's beauty, like that of many natural areas, is threatened. Climate change has already affected the park. Over the years, the Paradise-Stevens Glacier has shrunk as rising temperatures have caused it to melt. Climate change also affects what types of plants grow in different areas. This, in turn, changes where animals can live since they rely on specific plants for food and shelter.

Climate change is a serious issue. But it is not the only danger facing the park.

Mount Rainier's parking areas are often full.

People Problems

Mount Rainier's popularity is a challenge as well as a blessing. The park has had trouble managing the numbers of visitors. Roads and parking lots become overcrowded. Instead of being able to enjoy the outdoors, visitors can become stuck in a traffic jam.

Park rangers are working to reduce car traffic and are adding a shuttle, or bus, service. They also encourage people to visit at less crowded times.

Another challenge is keeping visitors safe.
Hikers may face deadly debris flows along rivers.
Sudden floods can occur when melting glacier lakes
burst open and flow out from the glacier. Rockfalls,
avalanches, and sudden changes in weather are
also dangerous and difficult to predict.

Park rangers work hard to provide up-to-date
information and warnings
about conditions.
Experienced guides are
available to lead climbing
groups. Everyone works
together to keep Mount
Rainier National Park
beautiful and safe. ★

Rescue workers practice using ropes
to rescue a person.

Map Mystery

In addition to its abundant natural wonders, Mount Rainier boasts many human-made points of interest. Follow these clues to find one of the most interesting places in the park.

Directions

1. Start at the park entrance named after a river on the eastern side of the park.

2. Head west to a visitor center named after a beautiful time of day.

3. Walk southwest to a glacier named after something in the kitchen.

4. Go south around the mountain until you reach a place named after Henry M. Jackson.

5. Keep going south until you reach Wonderland Trail. Follow it west and you'll find a fascinating museum.

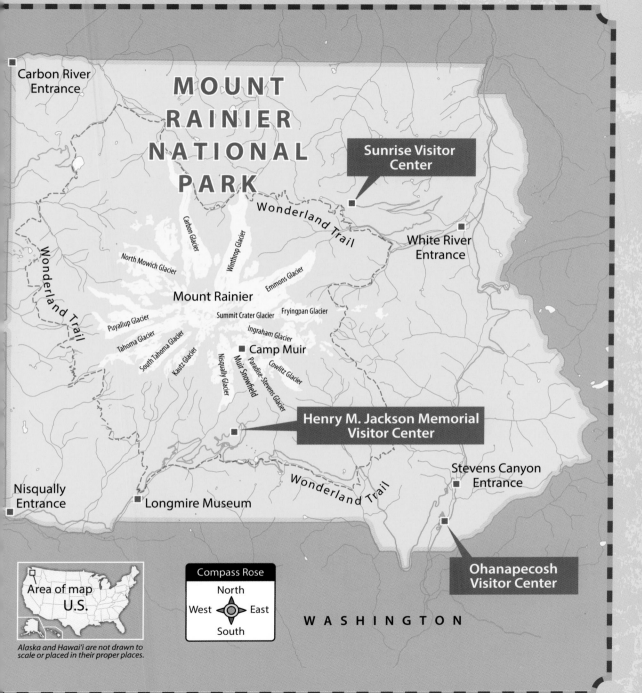

MOUNT RAINIER NATIONAL PARK

Carbon River Entrance

Sunrise Visitor Center

Wonderland Trail

White River Entrance

Carbon Glacier

North Mowich Glacier

Winthrop Glacier

Emmons Glacier

Wonderland Trail

Mount Rainier

Summit Crater Glacier

Fryingpan Glacier

Puyallup Glacier

Ingraham Glacier

Tahoma Glacier

South Tahoma Glacier

Kautz Glacier

Nisqually Glacier

Muir Snowfield

Paradise-Stevens Glacier

Cowlitz Glacier

● Camp Muir

Henry M. Jackson Memorial Visitor Center

Stevens Canyon Entrance

Nisqually Entrance

Longmire Museum

Wonderland Trail

Ohanapecosh Visitor Center

Area of map U.S.

Alaska and Hawai'i are not drawn to scale or placed in their proper places.

Compass Rose

North

West ✦ East

South

WASHINGTON

Be an Animal Tracker!

If you're ever in Mount Rainier National Park, keep an eye out for these animal tracks. They'll help you know which animals are in the area.

Mountain lion
Paw length: 3 inches (7.6 cm)

Fisher
Paw length: 2.5 inches (6.4 cm)

Coyote
Paw length: 2.5 inches (6.4 cm)

Bobcat
Paw length: 2 inches (5 cm)

Mountain goat
Hoof length: 3–4 inches (7.6–10 cm)

Beaver
Hind foot length: 6 inches (15.2 cm)

True Statistics

Length of the longest trail in the park: 93 mi. (150 km), Wonderland Trail

Number of major glaciers: 25

Number of people who tried to climb Mount Rainier in 2016: About 10,940

Percent of climbers who reached Mount Rainier's summit in 2016: 48

Number of rivers and streams: 470

Number of mammal species: 65

Number of bird species: About 187

Number of native fish species: 14

Number of reptile and amphibian species: 19

Number of plant species: More than 1,000

Did you find the truth?

(F) Peter Rainier named the park after himself.

(T) Some trees in the park are almost 1,000 years old.

Resources

Books

Flynn, Sarah Wassner, and Julie Beer. *National Parks Guide U.S.A.* Washington, DC: National Geographic, 2016.

Meinking, Mary. *What's Great About Washington?* Minneapolis: Lerner Publishing Group, 2015.

Tornio, Stacy. *Ranger Rick: National Parks!* Guilford, CT: Muddy Boots Press, 2016.

Visit this Scholastic website for more information on Mount Rainier National Park:

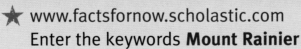 www.factsfornow.scholastic.com
Enter the keywords **Mount Rainier**

Important Words

alpine (AL-pine) of or relating to the high mountain ecosystem above where trees can grow

artifacts (AHR-tuh-fakts) objects made or changed by humans

composite volcano (kuhm-PAH-zit vahl-KAY-noh) a volcano built of layers of lava, ash, and other debris

conifers (KAH-nuh-furz) evergreen trees that produce their seeds in cones

debris (duh-BREE) the pieces of something that has been broken or destroyed

dormant (DOR-muhnt) resting or sleeping; describing a volcano that has not erupted in a long time but could erupt again

ecosystems (EE-koh-sis-tuhmz) groups of all the living things in a place and their relation to their environment

glaciers (GLAY-shurz) slow-moving masses of ice found in mountain valleys or polar regions

invasive (in-VAY-siv) of or having to do with entering a place in large numbers, usually with a negative effect

lahar (LAH-har) a flow of volcanic debris and melted snow

omnivores (AHM-nuh-vorz) animals that eat both plants and meat

predators (PREH-duh-turz) animals that live by hunting other animals for food